Mothe
to Vote

The Story of Elizabeth Cady Stanton

Jeri Cipriano

Boston, Massachusetts
Chandler, Arizona
Glenview, Illinois
Upper Saddle River, New Jersey

Illustrations
2, 3, 5, 6, 8, 9 Luigi Galante.

Photographs
Every effort has been made to secure permission and provide appropriate credit for photographic material.
The publisher deeply regrets any omission and pledges to correct errors called to its attention in subsequent editions.

Unless otherwise acknowledged, all photographs are the property of Pearson Education, Inc.

Photo locators denoted as follows: Top (T), Center (C), Bottom (B), Left (L), Right (R), Background (Bkgd)

All Photos: Library of Congress.

Copyright © 2013 by Pearson Education, Inc., or its affiliates. All rights reserved. Printed in the United States of America. This publication is protected by copyright, and permission should be obtained from the publisher prior to any prohibited reproduction, storage in a retrieval system, or transmission in any form by any means, electronic, mechanical, photocopying, recording, or likewise. For information regarding permissions, write to Pearson Curriculum Rights & Permissions, One Lake Street, Upper Saddle River, New Jersey 07458.

Pearson® is a trademark, in the U.S. and/or in other countries, of Pearson Inc. or its affiliates.

ISBN-13: 978-0-328-67700-9
ISBN-10:   0-328-67700-0

8 9 10 V0FL 16 15 14 13

Growing Up

Daniel Cady and Elizabeth Cady

On November 12, 1815, a daughter was born to Margaret and Daniel Cady of Johnstown, New York. They named the baby Elizabeth. The girl was expected to grow up to be like other women of the time. She would not be allowed to vote or have a career. She would not even be allowed to own property.

But Elizabeth Cady did not grow up to accept the ideas that people had then about women. Instead, she became a fighter for women's rights.

What made Cady challenge the people's expectations about women? When she was just 11 years old, one event changed her life. That year, her older brother Eleazar became ill and died. Elizabeth Cady's father was struck with grief. Cady later wrote that when she tried to comfort her father, Daniel Cady patted her and sighed, "Oh my daughter, I wish you were a boy."

The young daughter wanted to comfort her father. So she hugged him and replied, "I will try to be all my brother was!" And she did try. She learned how to ride horseback and became a fearless jumper. In school, she did as well as any boy. But Daniel Cady was not comforted. He still did not have a son.

Women in the 1800s

Elizabeth Cady's father was a successful lawyer and judge, and she enjoyed visiting him in his law office. She liked to listen in to the meetings he had. But what young Cady learned in these meetings sometimes shocked her.

She found out that women had few rights under the law. Only men were allowed to ask a court for a divorce, and women could not earn their own money. Their children and even their own belongings were considered to be their husband's property.

Elizabeth Cady also found that being a girl limited her opportunities for education. When she finished school, she had hoped to go on to the college that her brother attended. But it did not accept women. Most colleges admitted either men or women, but not both.

Daniel Cady made plans for his daughter to attend a women's college in Troy, New York. She was not happy about the decision. She understood that boys generally received a better education than girls did. In school, girls mostly learned skills that they would need to manage a house and care for children. Still, the college in Troy was better than most women's colleges, and Cady did well there. She graduated at age 18.

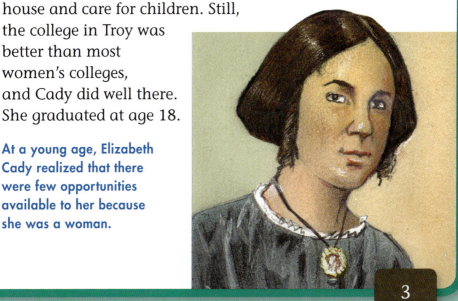

At a young age, Elizabeth Cady realized that there were few opportunities available to her because she was a woman.

Meeting Abolitionists

After graduation, Elizabeth Cady lived the life of a wealthy young woman of the time. She visited friends and attended parties. Her favorite activity was going to Peterboro, New York, to stay with her cousin Libby Smith. Smith's father, Gerrit, was an **abolitionist** who was working hard to end slavery.

Cady enjoyed being in the Smith home. There, she could participate in conversations about serious topics, such as justice and slavery. Such conversations did not generally take place in the Cady home. Many of the people who visited the Smiths talked about the **emancipation**, or freeing, of enslaved people. Cady loved these discussions and enjoyed talking to people who wanted to make a difference in the world.

Stanton's relative, Gerrit Smith, was a wealthy man who helped runaway slaves by selling portions of his land to them for just one dollar.

Henry Stanton was a good speaker. He was invited to be a representative at the World Anti-Slavery Convention in 1940.

Cady visited the Smith home often during the 1830s. There, she learned how to speak her mind and stand up for her beliefs. One of the Smith's guests, a man named Henry Stanton, was impressed with Cady. Stanton, an abolitionist, was ten years older than Cady. She was 24 when they met.

Cady and Stanton liked each other and enjoyed being together. When Stanton proposed marriage, Cady said yes. Her parents, however, were against the idea. They believed that Stanton was too old for their daughter. In addition, because they did not agree with the abolitionists' position on slavery, they disapproved of Stanton's work as an abolitionist.

Cady did not know what she should do. But then Stanton was invited to be a representative at the World Anti-Slavery Convention in London, England. Cady did not want to be apart from him. She agreed to marry Stanton and go with him to England.

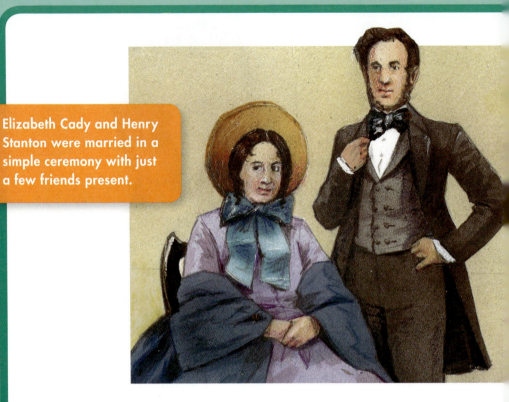

Elizabeth Cady and Henry Stanton were married in a simple ceremony with just a few friends present.

Marriage

Cady and Stanton were married on May 11, 1840. The wedding was not like other weddings of the time. Then, women promised to obey their husbands, but Elizabeth Cady would not make that promise. She also decided that she would not replace her name with her husband's name, as most wives did. Instead, she added Stanton's name to her own, calling herself Elizabeth Cady Stanton. At the time, this was very unusual.

Cady Stanton also shocked people when she did not address her husband in public as "Mr. Stanton," which was the practice back then. Instead, she called him by his first name, as people did only in the privacy of their own homes.

A New Friendship

In London, Elizabeth Cady Stanton met other American representatives to the World Anti-Slavery Convention. One representative was a woman from Philadelphia named Lucretia Mott.

As Stanton and Mott walked around London together, they talked about more than slavery. Stanton was happy to hear that Mott shared the same ideas she had about the rights of women. She was even more amazed to hear Mott speak so openly about her ideas. Stanton was impressed by Mott's intelligence and by how strongly she spoke about women's rights. Later, Stanton wrote that meeting Mott "opened to me a new world of thought."

Lucretia Mott in 1842

From Convention to Home

Though women were admitted to the World Anti-Slavery Convention, they were seated apart from the men. They were also told that they would not be allowed to speak. Stanton and Mott were outraged. They agreed then and there that one day they would have their own convention. It would be a convention for women's rights.

Elizabeth Cady Stanton had spent nearly six months overseas and was looking forward to seeing her family. Now that she was married, her father began to accept her husband. He invited the couple to live with the Cadys in Johnstown, New York, and even taught law to Henry Stanton.

After a year of living with her parents, Elizabeth and Henry Stanton moved to Boston, Massachusetts. Henry Stanton worked as a lawyer, and Elizabeth Cady Stanton became a mother. She gave birth to three boys between 1842 and 1845. Like other women of the time, Stanton cared for the children and the house. Her husband was busy with work and was not home often.

Elizabeth Cady Stanton and two of her sons in 1848

Seneca Falls, New York

In 1848, Elizabeth Cady Stanton received a letter from her friend Lucretia Mott. The Stanton family had by this time moved back to New York, to a town called Seneca Falls. Remembering their promise to each other in London, Mott invited Stanton to a meeting with four other women.

In the Declaration of Sentiments, Stanton wrote that, "all men and women are created equal."

The women Stanton met were all involved in the anti-slavery **movement**, but they believed that the problems women faced deserved their attention. They decided to hold a women's rights convention on July 19–20, 1848. Stanton reserved a meeting room in Seneca Falls and put an announcement in the local newspaper. The announcement described the event as "a convention to discuss the … condition and rights of women."

In preparation, the group drew up a statement of women's rights they called a Declaration of Sentiments. It was based on the Declaration of Independence that our country's founders signed in 1776. In the Declaration of Sentiments, the women listed their complaints. These included being denied an equal education and having no right to seek divorce. Stanton made sure they included a demand for women's **suffrage**, or the right to vote.

9

The names of those who signed the Declaration of Sentiments

The Women's Rights Convention

Both men and women attended the Women's Rights Convention. Even Frederick Douglass was one of the participants. Douglass was a well-known abolitionist who had been enslaved himself. At the convention, Lucretia Mott asked women in the audience to speak up and voice their opinion, even though it was not the custom at the time for women to do so.

Stanton read from the Declaration of Sentiments, and then she circulated it among the participants. In all, 68 women and 32 men signed the document to show that they supported the ideas within it.

Reaction to the Seneca Convention

News of the Seneca Convention spread. Soon, newspapers across the country printed articles that made fun of the convention and of what the women and men there were trying to achieve. Many of the Declaration signers were embarrassed and asked to have their names removed—even Cady Stanton's own sister! Frederick Douglass was one of the few people to publicly support the women in articles he wrote for his newspaper, *The North Star*.

Despite the criticisms, support for the declaration's ideas grew. **Petitions**, or written requests, for property rights and suffrage circulated. In the spring of 1850, women's rights conventions were held in several states. At each convention, Stanton was praised as a leader of the women's rights movement.

A New Style

One of the ideas in the women's rights movement was a call for more comfortable clothes. In the 1800s, women's dresses were made with up to 35 yards of fabric. They were so heavy and tight that some women had trouble breathing. Stanton's cousin, Libby Smith Miller, came up with a style of pants that women could wear. Amelia Bloomer called attention to the new style in a magazine she published. The pants became known as *bloomers*.

A Partnership with Susan B. Anthony

In 1851, Stanton met her lifelong friend and partner in the movement for women's rights, Susan B. Anthony. Anthony was a former schoolteacher who had also worked as an abolitionist. Three years later, the two women began working to change some New York state laws that restricted women's rights. Stanton had seven children and did not have the time that Anthony had to go to meetings. But Stanton was a good writer and wrote speeches that Anthony delivered before the New York **legislature**. Years later, Stanton wrote of her partnership with Susan B. Anthony: "I forged [made] the thunderbolts and she fired them."

Stanton (seated) and Anthony had a friendship and working partnership that lasted the rest of their lives.

In 1860, Stanton and Anthony convinced the New York legislature to pass new laws. These laws gave married women the right to have their own money and allowed mothers to keep their children after a divorce.

The National Campaign

After the Civil War, many changes took place. The fourteenth and fifteenth amendments gave rights and suffrage to African American men. But these rights continued to be denied to women. Stanton and Anthony thought this was unfair and continued working to change the laws so that women, too, would be allowed to vote.

In 1869, Elizabeth Cady Stanton and Susan B. Anthony decided to form an organization called the National Woman Suffrage Association (NWSA). The women also founded a women's rights newspaper called *The Revolution*. The newspaper's goal was to convince the public to support women's suffrage.

In Her Own Words

Elizabeth Cady Stanton wrote speeches that called for every human being—male and female—to have the same rights. In one speech, she explained why each person was responsible for himself or herself. "No matter how much women prefer to lean, to be protected and supported, nor how much men desire to have them do so, they must make the voyage of life alone." Therefore, women needed a say in all things that related to them—now and in their future.

The National Woman Suffrage Association was founded in 1869.

In 1872, Susan B. Anthony and 150 other women voted in the presidential election. Anthony and some of the others were arrested and found guilty of voting illegally. So Stanton and the NWSA proposed an amendment that would give women the right to vote. The amendment was introduced in the United States Congress in 1878 and each year after. But for 40 years, it did not get the votes in Congress that it needed to move to the state governments for voting. Approval from the states was necessary for the amendment to become law.

Elizabeth Cady Stanton worked hard for women's suffrage, but she had other goals besides getting women the right to vote. She wanted to help make life better for women everywhere. So throughout the 1870s, Stanton toured the country and gave speeches on women's rights. She also wrote many articles and later, worked on several books, including one with Susan B. Anthony about the movement the two of them had started.

Elizabeth Cady Stanton in 1902

After Stanton's death, the women's rights movement was carried on by others, like these women demanding suffrage in 1917.

Stanton Leads the Way

Elizabeth Cady Stanton died on October 26, 1902. After her death, one of her daughters found a letter she had written to President Theodore Roosevelt. Stanton had never had a chance to mail it. In the letter, Stanton urged the president to support women's suffrage.

Another 18 years went by before all women in the United States gained the right to vote. On August 18, 1920, the Nineteenth Amendment was passed, finally giving women the right to vote in national elections.

On November 2, 1920, more than eight million women voted for the first time in American history. Elizabeth Cady Stanton began the fight for women's rights and suffrage in 1848, but 72 years passed before women could vote. Many more years went by before women enjoyed the same rights and opportunities as men. And Elizabeth Cady Stanton had led the way.

Glossary

abolitionist a person who works to abolish, or end, slavery

amendment a change added to the United States Constitution

emancipation freeing from slavery

legislature the branch of government that makes laws

movement a group of people working together to bring about some result

petition a formal written request, signed by a number of people

suffrage the right to vote in elections